SPACE!

EARTH AND THE MOON

TERRY ALLAN HICKS

 **Marshall Cavendish**
Benchmark
New York

Marshall Cavendish Benchmark
99 White Plains Road
Tarrytown, New York 10591
www.marshallcavendish.us

All websites were available and accurate when this book was sent to press.

Library of Congress Cataloging-in-Publication Data
Earth and the moon / by Terry Allan Hicks.
    p. cm. -- (Space!)
Summary: "Describes Earth and its Moon, including their history, their composition,
and their roles in the solar system"--Provided by publisher.
Includes bibliographical references and index.
ISBN 978-0-7614-4254-7
1. Earth--Juvenile literature. 2. Moon--Juvenile literature. I. Title.
QB631.4.H53 2010
525--dc22
2009014663

Editor: Karen Ang
Publisher: Michelle Bisson
Art Director: Anahid Hamparian
Series Design by Daniel Roode
Production by nSight, Inc.

Front cover: A computer illustration of Earth and the Moon
Title page: *Apollo 11* astronaut Edwin "Buzz" Aldrin stands facing the American flag on
the Moon.
Photo research by Candlepants Inc.
Front cover: Donald E. Carroll / Getty Images
The photographs in this book are used by permission and through the courtesy of:
NASA: 1, 29; Tom Bridgman, GSFC Scientific Visualization Studio, 32, 33. Getty Images:
Paul & Lindamarie Ambrose, 4, 5; 6, 31, 46; Jim Ballard, 8; Time & Life Pictures, 22;
Pete Turner, 50; Kevin Kelley, 51; Tohoku Color Agency, 53. Photo Researchers Inc.: Mark
Garlick, 9, 14, 42; Steve Munsinger, 12; Chris Butler, 16; Larry Landolfi, 18, 19; Sheila Terry,
23; Omikron, 24; Detlev van Ravenswaay, 27; Gary Hincks, 34, 41; 37; Eckhard Slawik, 44.
AP Images: NASA, 30; Japan Aerospace Exploration Agency and NHK, HO, 38; Indian
Space Research Organization, HO, 48, 49; Japan Aerospace Exploration Agency, HO, 55.
Super Stock: Pixtal, 35, 36, 57. Shutterstock: 47. Image on page 11 by Mapping Specialists
© Marshall Cavendish Corporation.

Printed in Malaysia
123456

CONTENTS

1

A PLANET AND ITS MOON

arth is the largest **terrestrial** planet in the **Solar System**. It has a diameter of 7,926 miles (12,756 kilometers) and is a truly remarkable place. Earth is probably the only object in the Solar System capable of supporting life. It is certainly the only one that could support the complex system of billions of life-forms that we see everywhere around us. Some scientists even believe that Earth may be the only place in the entire **universe** where life exists.

One of the things that makes Earth so special is the planet's unique relationship with its one natural **satellite**, the Moon. Earth's powerful **gravity** locks the Moon in orbit around our planet. However, the Moon—even though it is much smaller—also has an extraordinary influence on Earth. The Moon affects the weather and the ocean tides. It is one of the factors that made all life on Earth, including human life, possible.

Until unmanned and manned spacecraft could travel to the Moon, people could only guess at what Earth looked like from its satellite.

Many other planets have multiple moons, but Earth has only one. Venus and Mercury, however, do not have any moons at all.

Earth's Moon is not the only **moon** in the Solar System. There are at least 166 moons circling planets in the Solar System. Jupiter, the largest of the eight planets, has at least sixty-two moons, and it is possible that more are waiting to be discovered. Our Moon is also far from being the largest. (One of Jupiter's moons, Ganymede, is actually larger than the planet Mercury.) However, Earth's Moon is the fifth-largest moon in the Solar System. When comparing planets and their moons, our Moon has the greatest size and greatest **mass** compared to the planet it orbits. Its closeness to Earth means that even this amount of mass (1.2 percent of Earth's) has an extremely powerful influence on us.

THE BEGINNINGS OF THE UNIVERSE

Earth and the Moon and the rest of the Solar System make up just one very small part of the universe. The section of the universe that **astronomers**, **physicists**, and other scientists have been able to see using special telescopes and other sensitive instruments measures about 28 billion **light-years** across. Most scientists agree that the universe is far larger than that. They think that the universe is constantly expanding—or always growing larger— and that it may actually be infinite, without any end at all.

For many years, scientists have been trying to understand how the universe came into existence. The most commonly held view today is what is known as the Big Bang theory. This theory states that about 13.7 billion years ago, there was a sudden huge expansion of space. When this extremely violent process ended,

LIGHT-YEARS

The light-year is a unit created especially to measure the huge distances in space. Scientists believe that nothing can move faster than the speed of light, which moves through empty space at a rate of about 186,000 miles (300,000 km) per second. A light-year is the distance—about 5.9 trillion miles (9.5 trillion km)—that light travels in one Earth year.

matter began to appear. Some of this matter formed into **stars**, which are huge balls of flaming gas that spin in space and give off enormous amounts of energy in the form of light, heat, and **radiation**.

Over millions and millions of years, these stars began to come together in huge revolving clusters of stars and other matter called **galaxies**. Scientists have identified hundreds of millions of galaxies, many of them with trillions of stars in them. Our galaxy is known as the Milky Way, and even though it is not a particularly large or significant galaxy, it has hundreds of billions of stars. One of those stars is the one we call the Sun.

Part of the Milky Way can be seen stretching across a starlit night sky.

THE SOLAR SYSTEM

The Sun is not an especially large or bright star, but it is the largest object in the Solar System. It is six hundred times larger than everything else in the Solar System put together. (The Solar System is named for the Sun, which in Latin is called Sol. *Solar* means "of the Sun.") The Sun also has more than 99 percent of all the mass in the Solar System. This is why it exerts the gravitational force that holds billions of **celestial objects** locked in orbit around it. The Sun is also the most important source of energy in the Solar System. It produces the light and heat that affect even the most distant objects in the Solar System.

Most scientists believe that the Solar System was created about 4.56 billion years ago. They think a huge cloud of gas and dust at the edge of the Milky Way began to form, perhaps in the aftermath of the explosion of a nearby star. The cloud's gravitational force slowly brought the gases and dust particles together, causing them to become hotter and, eventually, to explode. This explosion created the Sun.

The Beginnings of the Planets

The force of this huge explosion also sent gas and dust particles flying far out into space. But they remained captured by the Sun's gravitational force and eventually formed into a ring that

The Sun started out as a circular disc that slowly bulged outward from its center. Rocks, dust, gases, and other material in space orbited the Sun, colliding and crashing until they formed planets and other celestial bodies.

revolved around the Sun. Very slowly, in a process that probably took at least 100,000 years, particles of matter came together in **planetesimals,** which are small bodies that eventually became the planets and many of the billions of other objects that now circle the Sun.

The four terrestrial planets—Mercury, Venus, Earth, and Mars—are relatively small and made mostly of metallic rock. This is because they were close to the Sun's intense heat, which did not allow significant amounts of ice or gas to form. The four outer planets, which were not exposed to as much heat from the Sun, were able to draw greater amounts of liquid and gas to them. These so-called gas giants formed over a much longer period and became much larger than the inner planets.

THE EARTH IS BORN

Earth is the largest of the inner planets. Our planet, like all the others, orbits the Sun in an **elliptical** path. Earth is about 93 million miles (149.6 million km) away from the Sun. And like all the other planets, Earth rotates at an angle, called an **axial tilt,** in relation to its orbit around the Sun. This axial tilt—Earth's is a constant 32.5 degrees—together with the rotation of Earth on its **axis,** is responsible for the changes in the seasons and for many other factors that affect everyday life on Earth.

When Earth first formed, the entire planet was probably hot and liquid. As Earth slowly cooled, a mostly metallic core, made

Earth is often called the third rock from the Sun because of its closeness to the Sun and the rocky material that it is made of. Of the other planets shown here, Pluto is the only one that is not considered a regular planet. As of 2006, Pluto was reclassified as a dwarf planet.

up largely of iron and nickel, was left behind. This core was surrounded by a rocky crust that slowly hardened to become the planet's surface. During the billions of years that followed, Earth changed greatly. A huge continent, called Pangaea, began to form and then its pieces very slowly began to break and drift apart, creating the continents that exist today.

Volcanic eruptions, earthquakes, and other forces from beneath Earth's surface formed mountains, valleys, plains, and

Scientists believe that a young Earth would have been completely uninhabitable by humans. The extreme heat from falling meteorites and spewing lava and the shifting land would have made life impossible.

EARTH AND VENUS

Venus is often called Earth's sister planet because it is the closest in size and weight to Earth. This does not mean that humans could survive on Venus. Any Earth life-form that visited Venus would be crushed by Venus's air pressure, suffocated by toxic gases, and burned by the intense temperatures. Some scientists call Venus "Earth's evil twin." However, many believe that studying Venus may help us to learn more about Earth's origins and how to solve human-made problems, such as pollution, that could lead to planetary conditions similar to those on Venus.

many of the other features we know on Earth's surface today. Forces from space—especially collisions with **asteroids** and other objects—also left their mark on the young Earth. Eventually, water and an **atmosphere**—the factors that are most important to the emergence of life—began to appear. But Earth continued to evolve, and it is still evolving today.

THE MAKING OF THE MOON

Scientists have many conflicting ideas about the Moon's origins. Some believe that Earth and the Moon were formed at the same time, by the explosion that created the Sun and everything else in the Solar System. Others think the Moon was an already-formed

An illustration shows how the Moon probably formed. Theia collided with Earth (top left) causing a lot of debris to orbit the planet (center) until gravity formed the Moon (bottom right).

celestial object that was simply captured by Earth's gravity. But the view that is most commonly accepted today is the Theia, or giant impact, theory.

According to this theory, a large celestial object about the size of Mars, which scientists have named Theia, collided with Earth about 4.5 billion years ago. It bounced off the planet, taking with it an enormous amount of matter from Earth. This matter—a huge cloud of rock, dust, and gas from both Earth and Theia—formed into a ring around the planet, held in place by the planet's gravity. The individual particles of matter in the ring had gravity of their own, and they eventually combined into a single body, which continued to collect more and more matter. This created the Moon, which is 2,160 miles (3,476 km) in diameter. However the Moon was created, it is clear that its origins are closely linked to Earth's. The Moon rocks the astronauts brought back with them are roughly the same age as those on Earth and have many characteristics in common with them.

The young Moon was clearly affected by extremely violent forces. For about 750 million years, the Moon was struck over and over again by meteorites and asteroids. The force of these strikes created many of the **impact craters**, cracks, and other features that can be seen on the Moon's surface. More than 500,000 craters can be seen from Earth. Eventually, there were fewer of these space collisions. Then a long period of intense volcanic activity began. Many of the Moon's craters were filled

When the Moon was first forming, it probably had active volcanoes and underground lava that shaped and carved up the satellite's surface.

with lava, which is molten volcanic rock that emerged from deep beneath the surface. When the lava cooled, it became solid rock and formed the flat, dark areas on the Moon's surface that are called **maria**. The lighter, raised areas surrounding the maria are known as the lunar highlands.

Then, about 3.2 billion years ago, the volcanic activity simply stopped. Since that time, the Moon—unlike Earth—has essentially been "dead." However, this does not mean that the Moon has not changed in that time. Its surface continues to be marked, scarred, and changed by the impacts of objects from space. Some of the most visible impact craters are among the youngest. Copernicus, a crater 57 miles (91 km) wide and 2.3 miles (3.7 km) deep, was probably created by a massive asteroid strike about 900 million years ago. The slightly smaller Tycho crater, near the Moon's south pole, probably formed about 100 million years ago.

Today, the Moon is still the only celestial object besides Earth that human beings have visited. It is probably the one we know the most about, but there is much that we still do not know. There are questions about the Moon that human beings have been asking for hundreds, perhaps thousands, of years—questions that still remain to be answered.

2

EARTH AND THE MOON THROUGH THE AGES

For as long as human beings have lived on Earth, we have been trying to understand the planet and its place in the universe. Astronomers and other observers have been watching and recording the movements of the Sun, the Moon, the other planets, and the stars for at least six thousand years. Many prehistoric ruins, such as Europe's mysterious Stonehenge and the Mayan pyramids of Central America, were probably early **observatories** used to follow the movements of heavenly bodies—especially the Moon.

Even the earliest people seem to have understood the close relationship between the movements of the Moon, its changing

Even before telescopes and other astronomy equipment was invented, people were fascinated by the changing Moon.

"face," and the rising and falling of the ocean tides. People from ancient times also recognized that the movements of the Moon could be used to create an accurate calendar. This was extremely important for people who lived off the land and the sea—for example, hunters, farmers, and fishermen—and needed to be able to predict changing natural conditions.

ANCIENT EYES WATCHING THE MOON

The first written records of astronomical observations are found on thousands of clay tablets left by the Assyrians—an ancient Middle Eastern people—almost three thousand years ago. Their records and those of many other ancient peoples were very precise. However, over the centuries, astronomers in many different places continued to seek ways to make their observations of the sky even more accurate.

The ancient Chinese had a lunar calendar and used observations to predict one of the most mysterious, most beautiful, and most feared of all the phenomena caused by the movements of the Moon—the **eclipse**. The Moon plays an important role in the myths, legends, and religious beliefs of people all over the world. The ancient Romans called their moon goddess Luna, and it is from her name that we get the word

ECLIPSES

Throughout the ages, eclipses—times when the Sun or the Moon is partially or completely blocked from view—have been seen as signs that great change is coming. Many ancient peoples actually thought an eclipse meant the end of the world. The ancient Chinese believed that an eclipse occurred when a dragon swallowed the Sun or the Moon. Even today, it is a Chinese tradition to bang on pots and pans during an eclipse, to make noise to scare the dragon away.

lunar, which means "of the Moon." (Luna's mother was called Theia, which is why scientists chose that name for the celestial body that may have "given birth" to the Moon.) The Greeks and many other ancient people thought of the moon goddess as a huntress. The ancients often showed Luna—called Selene by the Greeks and by many other names, as well—riding across the night sky in a silver chariot. In other traditions, such as the Japanese religion of Shinto, it is the Moon who is hunted by her brother the Sun.

People have always thought the Moon affected human behavior and destiny. The word *lunatic,* for someone who is acting very strangely, comes from the Roman name for the Moon. It reflects

The ancient Roman Moon goddess is shown traveling across the night sky in her chariot.

the widely held view that the Moon—especially the full Moon—causes madness. Many people believe that evil spirits wander the earth when the Moon is full. Another myth about the full Moon involves humans turning into werewolves. Even today, many people still believe that people's behavior becomes strange when there is a full Moon.

A NEW VIEW OF THE HEAVENS

For thousands of years, most people believed in the geocentric, or Earth-centered, view of the universe. This view—sometimes called the Ptolemaic system, for the ancient Greek-Egyptian astronomer Ptolemy—stated that the Sun, the Moon, and the stars were all perfect spheres circling Earth. But in 1543, a book by the Polish astronomer Nicolaus Copernicus presented a radically different view of the universe—the heliocentric, or Sun-centered, system. Copernicus believed Earth and all the other planets actually orbited the Sun. His views were extremely

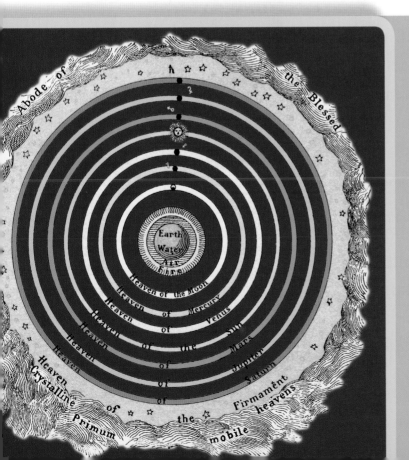

Most people once believed that Earth was the center of the Solar System. This illustration shows the Ptolemaic system along with the five other planets (Mercury, Venus, Mars, Jupiter, and Saturn) that were known at the time.

controversial and were not widely accepted for many years, but later astronomers proved him right.

One of those astronomers was an Italian scientist named Galileo Galilei. Beginning in 1609, he used a telescope to study the surface of the Moon. His careful observations of the way the shadows on the Moon changed over time proved that the Moon was not a perfect sphere. It also proved that its surface was covered with mountains and valleys, just like Earth's. Galileo used his studies to create the first accurate drawings of the Moon's surface. Of course, like all Moon watchers before the twentieth century, he could see only one side of the Moon, the one that permanently faces Earth. In the mid-seventeenth century, two more Italian astronomers, Giovanni Battista Riccioli and Francesco Maria Grimaldi, drew the first true map of the surface of the Moon. They gave the different features names—many of which are still familiar today.

Though his telescope was nowhere near as strong as telescopes of today, Galileo's sketches of the Moon's surface were very detailed. He was able to see many of the craters and other markings.

THE DARK SIDE OF THE MOON

The Moon orbits Earth in a fixed—or synchronous—rotation, which means that the same side always faces our planet. For this reason, the far or "dark" side of the Moon was invisible to people on Earth until modern times. However, because of a phenomenon called libration, which is a kind of wobbling effect caused by the Moon's irregular orbit, observers on Earth can actually see a total of about 59 percent of the Moon's surface over the course of a month.

People have always had strange ideas about the Moon, some of them serious, some of them fanciful. Many children all over the world grow up believing they can see the face of the Man in the Moon, and the silly idea that the Moon is made of cheese has somehow lasted for more than four hundred years. In the summer of 1835, the *New York Sun* reported that life had been found on the Moon. The newspaper said the famous British astronomer Sir John Herschel, using a powerful new telescope, had seen blue unicorns, herds of bison, and even human beings with wings! The story, which has come to be known as the Great Moon Hoax, was quickly exposed as a fake, but not before thousands of people had been fooled.

As people's knowledge of the Moon grew, so did their fascination with it. The idea of traveling to the Moon has been found in works of art for hundreds of years, and it was the subject of some of the first science fiction stories. The French writer Jules Verne's famous book *From the Earth to the Moon* imagined a rocket making a Moon voyage in 1865—almost exactly a century before it became a reality. One of the earliest silent films, *A Trip to the Moon,* showed space travelers finding many strange creatures on the Moon—after their rocket hits the Man in the Moon in the eye!

THE SPACE RACE

By the middle of the twentieth century, the invention of powerful long-distance rockets was beginning to make space travel a real possibility. In the late 1950s, the United States and its then-rival, the Soviet Union, began the space race, which was a competition to see which nation could explore space first. The two nations sent satellites into orbit around Earth, and then manned spacecraft. But the most important goal of this competition was to be the first to reach the Moon.

The Soviet Union got a head start in 1959, beginning a long series of unmanned expeditions, all called *Luna,* focusing largely on exploring the far side of the Moon. The second of the *Luna* spacecraft was the first ever to land on the Moon, but it was destroyed on impact. *Luna 3* sent back the first images anyone had ever seen of the Moon's dark side.

On May 25, 1961, the country's new president, John F. Kennedy, gave a famous speech in which he said, "I believe that this nation should commit itself to achieving the goal, before this decade is out, of landing a man on the Moon and returning him safely to the Earth." This was an extraordinary idea because at that time, the United States—unlike the Soviet Union—had not yet even succeeded in placing a manned spacecraft in orbit around the Earth. Only a little more than a month earlier, on April 12, the Soviet Union had sent the first human being—Yuri Gagarin—into space.

Computer artwork shows what *Luna I* probably looked like in 1959 when it passed near the Moon.

The **National Aeronautics and Space Administration (NASA)**, the United States government's space exploration agency, began preparing for the difficult, expensive, and dangerous task of sending human beings to the Moon. NASA sent several series of unmanned spacecraft to study the surface of the Moon to try to learn what conditions awaited the astronauts who would land there. The *Ranger* spacecraft were sent to crash-land on the Moon, the *Orbiter* missions photographed the Moon from orbit, looking for landing places, and the *Surveyor* spacecraft made "soft" landings to find out what the lunar surface was like.

Meanwhile, NASA was building and testing more and more powerful rockets and learning how to send human beings into space. On May 5, 1961, the *Mercury* program had succeeded in sending an American astronaut, Alan Shepard, into space and bringing him back to Earth. That mission did not go into orbit around the Earth, as Gagarin's had. But on February 20, 1962, astronaut John Glenn circled the planet three times before "splashing down" in the Atlantic Ocean.

The *Mercury* missions showed that NASA could put an astronaut in space, and the *Gemini* program, which followed, demonstrated that the agency could take on longer missions with more than one astronaut. These programs laid the foundation for the *Apollo* missions, which would first approach and study the Moon and then land human beings on its surface. The *Apollo 8, 9,* and *10* missions—launched between December 1968 and May 1969—all carried astronauts close to the Moon, but they were not designed to land there.

The First Steps on the Moon

The first manned mission to the Moon, *Apollo 11,* was launched from Cape Canaveral on July 16, 1969. A huge rocket lifted off, carrying three astronauts in a two-part spacecraft: a command and services module, called *Columbia,* which would orbit the Moon, and the lunar module, called *Eagle,* which would actually travel to the Moon's surface. When Earth's gravitational force

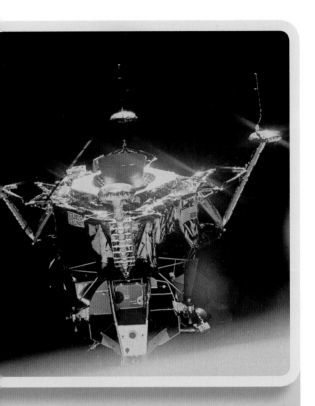

This picture was taken after *Apollo II*'s lunar module, *Eagle,* separated from the *Columbia* and headed toward the Moon's surface.

had been left behind, the spacecraft detached itself from the rocket and continued on its way. Three days later, it slipped into orbit around the Moon.

One of the astronauts, Michael Collins, stayed behind to pilot *Columbia*. But Neil Armstrong and Buzz Aldrin entered the tiny lunar module and ascended to a safe landing on the Sea of Tranquility, radioing back, "The Eagle has landed." Six hours later, Neil Armstrong stepped outside the lunar module and began his lunar walk, saying, "That's one small step for man, one giant leap for mankind." Many historians and scientists believe that this moment represented the most important scientific achievement in the history of the human race.

Both Armstrong and Aldrin walked on the Moon, collected space rocks, performed scientific experiments, and spoke on the telephone with the president of the United States. After

Astronaut James Irwin salutes the flag as he stands on the Moon's surface in 1971. Irwin was part of the *Apollo 15* mission, which used a lunar module (center) and a lunar rover (right), which would travel across parts of the Moon.

about twenty-one hours, they returned to *Eagle* and blasted off from the Moon's surface, heading back to *Columbia,* which was waiting to carry them back to Earth.

Six more *Apollo* missions to the Moon followed. In all, twelve people—all of them Americans—have walked on the surface of the Moon. (Some of the later *Apollo* missions also used **rovers**, small motorized vehicles also called "Moon buggies," to travel across the lunar surface.) But by the early 1970s, NASA and its

Moon program were suffering from lack of money and declining public interest in space travel. The last manned spacecraft to land on the Moon was *Apollo 17* in December 1972. The three *Apollo* missions that had been scheduled to follow it were canceled. The Soviet Union also seemed to lose interest in the Moon. It never tried to send humans there, and its last unmanned *Luna* mission was in 1976.

Space travel has continued, with astronauts living in space for long periods—on space stations orbiting Earth—and unmanned spacecraft exploring the outer reaches of the Solar System. But in the decades since the *Apollo 17* mission, human beings have not set foot on the Moon even once. And until very recently, it seemed entirely possible that they never would again.

This striking image of Earth was taken during the last *Apollo* mission, *Apollo 17*, in 1972.

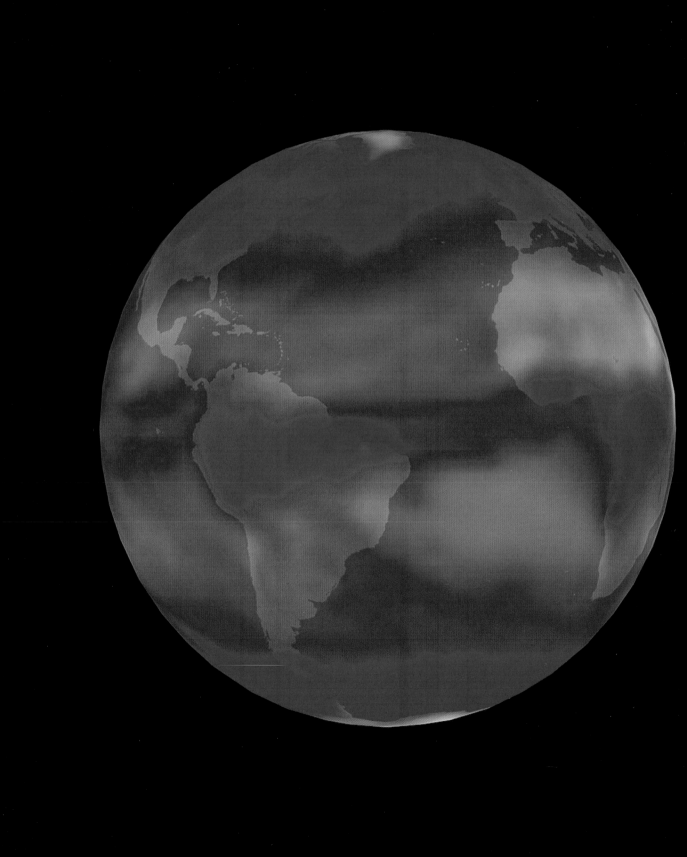

3

A CLOSER LOOK AT EARTH AND THE MOON

EARTH FROM THE INSIDE OUT

he center of Earth is an inner core, about 1,490 miles (2,400 km) in diameter. This inner core, which is made up of solid iron and nickel, is extremely hot, with a temperature of about 6650 degrees Fahrenheit (3677 degrees Celsius). Its intense heat has a powerful effect on the next two layers and beyond. An outer core, which is also made of iron and nickel—but in molten form—is about 1,430 miles (2,300 km) thick. Beyond that is the Earth's mantle, a layer of mostly **silicate** rock that is about 1,740 miles (2,800 km) thick. The matter in the outer core and the mantle is

This computerized image of Earth was taken by special instruments onboard the *Terra* satellite, which is orbiting above the planet. The special image shows the amounts of heat different parts of the planet release back into space.

constantly in motion because of the heat from the inner core. This movement probably creates the Earth's powerful magnetic field, known as the **magnetosphere**, which reaches far out into space.

The layer of Earth at and just below the surface is known as the crust. This area, which ranges from 4 to 25 miles (6 to 40 km) in depth, is also made up mostly of metallic substances called silicates. Covering more than 70 percent of the Earth's surface is the feature that truly sets the Earth apart from all the other bodies in the Solar System—huge amounts of water. Other

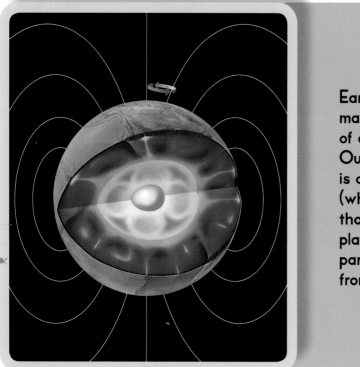

Earth is made up of many interior layers of different materials. Outside its surface, is a magnetosphere (white circular lines) that help to protect the planet from dangerous particles and radiation from the Sun.

planets and moons, including Earth's, either have some water or had some in the past, but none have had the extraordinary amount found on Earth.

Another aspect of the Earth that helps make it unique is its atmosphere. Other planets have atmospheres—and at least one moon, Titan, which orbits Saturn has one—but those planets' atmospheres are all poisonous to us. As far as scientists have been able to tell today, only Earth has the oxygen- and nitrogen-rich atmosphere that is capable of supporting life. Earth's atmosphere extends about 310 miles (499 km) from the planet's surface.

The atmosphere, which also includes argon, oxygen, carbon dioxide, and other gases, performs other extremely important functions. The atmosphere filters out much of the Sun's radiation, including particles in the **solar wind,**

One of Earth's nicknames is The Blue Planet, because of the amount of water it has. This satellite image was taken above the Indian Ocean.

Clouds, storms, and other weather events in Earth's atmosphere can be seen from space. This image shows Hurricane Linda as it churns over the Atlantic Ocean.

which can be extremely harmful to life. Earth's atmosphere also burns up asteroids and **meteoroids** before they reach the surface of Earth, where they could do a great deal of damage. If not for the atmosphere, the planet's heat would escape to outer space and Earth's climate would not be stable. All of these factors are essential to maintaining life on Earth.

A PLANET IN DANGER

The atmosphere protects life on Earth in another important way, known as the "greenhouse gas effect." Some of the gases in the atmosphere, including carbon dioxide and water vapor, trap some of the Sun's heat. Without the greenhouse gas effect, Earth's temperature might be as much as 60 degrees Fahrenheit (16 degrees C) lower, making life difficult, if not impossible, for human beings and other life-forms. However, in recent years, temperatures on Earth have actually risen dramatically. It is now widely believed that the increase in global temperatures is caused by pollution that releases huge amounts of gases—especially carbon dioxide—into the atmosphere. This overabundance of greenhouse gases causes global warming, which is melting the polar ice caps, raising sea levels worldwide, and having many other damaging effects on Earth and its inhabitants. Venus experiences a similar greenhouse gas effect in its atmosphere. Scientists hope that learning about Venus's atmosphere may help them solve global warming problems on Earth.

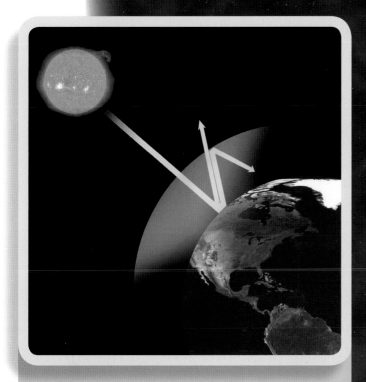

Too much greenhouse gas in Earth's atmosphere can trap dangerous amounts of heat and radiation, which then damage the planet.

THE MOON FROM THE INSIDE OUT

The Moon's internal structure and composition is, in some ways, very similar to Earth's. A small inner core of rock, with a temperature of 2700 degrees Fahrenheit (1482 degrees C), may be completely or partially molten. The next layer is an outer core, made of semisolid rock. Beyond that is a solid mantle that is about 600 miles (966 km) thick. Next is the crust, a layer covered with loose, dusty rock known as **regolith**. One of the main

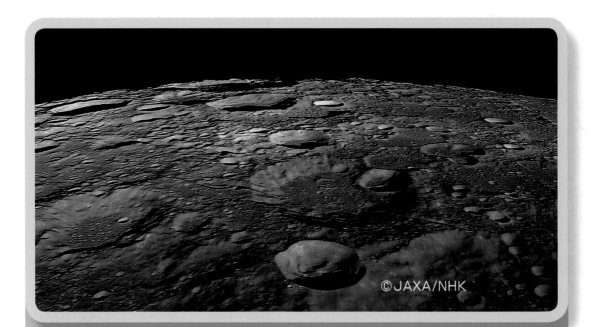

©JAXA/NHK

In 2007, special high-definition (HDTV) cameras onboard a Japanese Moon probe took these very clear images of the Moon's surface.

concerns of the first lunar missions was whether spacecraft would sink into the regolith, but the *Apollo 11* astronauts found that it was quite firm and stable. Later missions discovered beautiful volcanic Moon glass, in colors ranging from green to red, in the regolith.

The Moon's crust is a different thickness on the two sides of the Moon. The crust on the near side, the side that is visible from Earth, is only about 40 miles (64 km) deep. On the far, or dark, side of the Moon, the crust is about 60 miles (97 km) deep. Despite all the knowledge we have gained about the Moon, we still do not really know the reason for these differences.

The main features of the lunar surface are the maria, the highlands, and the many impact craters. Forces both from outside and inside have left other marks on the Moon. For example, the Lunar Apennines—a mountain range formed by the impact that created the Mare Imbrium, one of the Moon's great "seas"— follows a curving line more than 1.9 miles (3 km) long and rising more than 1.9 miles (3 km) in height. The Copernicus Crater has mountains inside it that are 8 miles (5 km) high—that is far taller than Mount Everest, the tallest mountain on Earth, which is only 5.5 miles (8.8 km) in height. Great cliffs, such as the Rupes Altai, tower more than 1.1 miles (1.8 km) above the surface.

The temperature on the Moon's surface varies much more widely than Earth's. The temperature is about 225 degrees Fahrenheit (107 degrees C) during the day and -307 degrees Fahrenheit

(-153 degrees C) at night. Such huge temperature swings would probably make it impossible for life to develop on the Moon, even if there was enough of an atmosphere to support it. Most people think of the Moon as having no atmosphere, but it actually has an extremely thin atmosphere made up mostly of tiny amounts of gases, including neon, helium, and hydrogen, as well as water.

A CELESTIAL DANCE

What truly sets Earth and the Moon apart from all the other objects in the Solar System is their complex relationship with each other, and with the Sun. Their movements through space create many of the things we take for granted—the days, the months, the years, the seasons, even the weather.

Days, Years, and Seasons

Earth, like all the other planets, orbits the Sun in a regular but elliptical path. Earth takes 365.25 days—the period we define as a year—to travel once around the Sun. (Other planets take much longer. Saturn's orbit, for example, lasts 29.5 years.) Earth's path around the Sun is not a perfect circle, but is an ellipse, which means that Earth's distance from the Sun varies at different times. This distance can range from 91 million miles (146 million km) to 94.5 million miles (152 million km).

Earth also rotates on its axis, an invisible line that runs through the planet from the North Pole to the South Pole. As

The Moon orbits Earth, and together, they both orbit the Sun along with other planets and moons in the Solar System.

the planet turns, one side is always in light, the other always in darkness. This is why we have day and night on Earth. To an observer standing on Earth, the Sun seems to be moving across the sky, rising in the east and setting in the west. But what is really happening is that the planet is turning—in a counterclockwise direction, if seen from a point above the North Pole—creating day and night.

Also like the other planets, Earth faces the Sun at an angle. This angle, called the axial tilt, is a constant 23.5 degrees. This tilt is responsible for the changing seasons. The tilt remains constant throughout the year. So at different times, sunlight strikes different parts of Earth differently. Between December and March, the Northern Hemisphere receives mostly indirect light, much of it filtered through the atmosphere, so it is winter there. The period when the Northern Hemisphere is in light is shorter, and the period of darkness is longer. In the Southern Hemisphere, this phenomenon is reversed, so when it is winter in New York, it is summer in Buenos Aires, Argentina. In the equatorial zone, where direct light strikes the Earth regularly throughout the year, the land is hot most of the time and there is little seasonal variation.

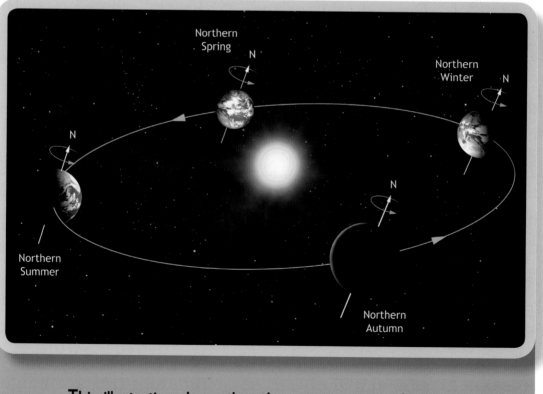

This illustration shows that the seasons come about because Earth spins on its axis as it orbits the Sun.

Solstices and Equinoxes

Twice a year, direct sunlight strikes the Earth at its farthest north and south points. These days are called the **solstices**. The summer solstice comes on June 20 or 21, when the Northern Hemisphere is tilted closest to the Sun. This gives the northern part of the planet its longest period of daylight and marks the beginning of summer. The winter solstice, on December 21 or 22, marks the beginning of winter in the Northern Hemisphere, with the shortest period of daylight. (The opposite is happening south of the equator.)

Twice a year, the periods of light and darkness are exactly equal. These are called the **equinoxes** (from a Latin word that means "equal night"). The vernal equinox, on March 20 or 21 every year, marks the beginning of spring in the Northern Hemisphere. The autumnal equinox, on September 22 or 23, marks the beginning of autumn north of the equator. In the Southern Hemisphere, the seasons are exactly reversed.

Phases of the Moon

The Moon is also moving through space, revolving around Earth and rotating on its own axis. Interestingly, each of these processes takes exactly the same amount of time—27.3 days. This rotation is the reason the Moon always shows roughly the same side to an observer on Earth. But as anyone who has ever

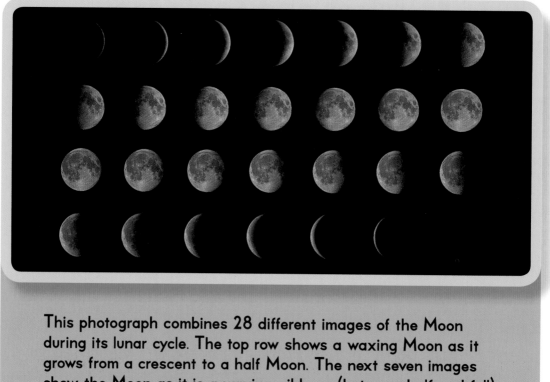

This photograph combines 28 different images of the Moon during its lunar cycle. The top row shows a waxing Moon as it grows from a crescent to a half Moon. The next seven images show the Moon as it is a waxing gibbous (between half and full) that leads to a full Moon. After the full Moon, the cycle begins its waning phase, during which the Moon seems to shrink in size.

looked up at the night sky knows, the Moon's "face" is constantly changing. This is because the Moon has no light of its own, only the reflected light from the Sun. To an observer on Earth, this light seems to strike different parts of the satellite at different times. These are the periods we know as the phases of the Moon.

This process, known as the **lunar cycle** begins when the Sun, Earth, and Moon are all aligned, with the Moon's lighted side completely facing the Sun, so that the Moon cannot be seen from Earth at all. Then the Moon's lighted side begins to appear, a little more each night. This is known as the period of the waxing (or increasing) Moon. As the Moon moves through the waxing phase, a waxing crescent Moon—the slender curving shape we all know so well—appears. The point when we can see half of the lighted side of the Moon is called the first-quarter Moon. Within a few days, three quarters of the lighted side can be seen from Earth, and this point is known as the waxing gibbous Moon. A few days later, the entire lighted side of the Moon is visible. This is the period that is called the full Moon.

After the full Moon, the process begins again, but in reverse. This is the waning (decreasing) period, with the Moon passing through the waning gibbous, third-quarter, and waning crescent phases. The lunar cycle takes 29.5 days—about the period we know as a month—to complete. This is, once again, because the Moon is not alone in its movements. At the same time it is revolving around Earth, Earth is also orbiting the Sun.

Eclipses

The movements of the Sun, Earth, and Moon are also responsible for eclipses. All celestial objects (except stars) cast shadows, and an eclipse happens when one celestial object moves into another's shadow, completely or partially blocking it from view.

When a **lunar eclipse** occurs, the Sun, Earth, and Moon align in space, with Earth positioned precisely between the Sun and Moon. The Sun slowly disappears into Earth's shadow, until it is partially or completely hidden, for a period ranging from a few minutes to almost four hours. A partial eclipse is quite common, usually occurring at least twice a year, but a total eclipse is much more rare. A lunar eclipse can happen only during a full Moon, but it does not occur during every full Moon, because of the varying axial tilts of Earth and the Moon.

A **solar eclipse** occurs when the Moon passes directly between the Sun and the Earth, blocking the Sun from view, partially or totally, for a period ranging from a few minutes to as much as two hours. Partial eclipses of the Sun, like those of the Moon, are much more common than total eclipses. During a total solar eclipse, only the hazy atmosphere around the Sun can be seen, and the entire surface of the Earth goes

During this lunar eclipse in March 2007, the Moon took on a reddish color.

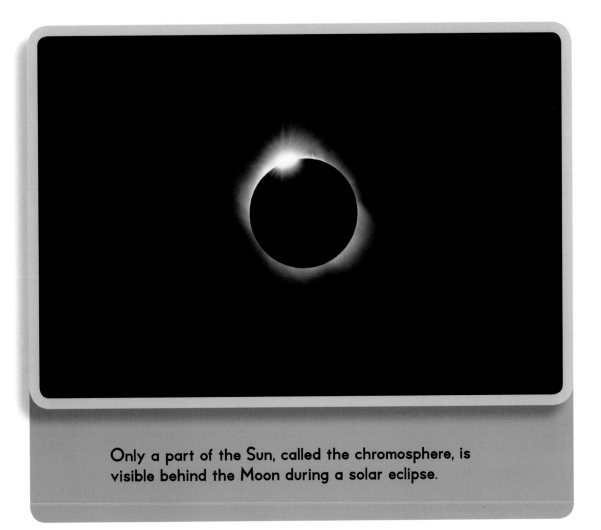

Only a part of the Sun, called the chromosphere, is visible behind the Moon during a solar eclipse.

dark. It is easy to understand why ancient people who could not predict eclipses might have thought it meant the end of the world, and why people have since tried to understand the place of Earth and the Moon in the heavens.

4
BACK TO THE MOON AND BEYOND

Earth is unique in the Solar System and some of the scientists who study space suspect that our planet may actually be the only one of its kind in the entire universe. We may never know because of the enormous distances in space, but we do know that there are many factors that make Earth very unusual.

One thing that made life possible on Earth is the type of star it orbits. If the Sun was bigger and hotter, life—especially complex life—would probably not have been able to emerge or survive on our planet. Another factor in the emergence of life on Earth was the planet's position. The planets closer to the Sun—Mercury and Venus—are probably too hot to support life as we know it.

This October 2008 launch photograph of the rocket that is carrying *Chandrayaan-I* to the Moon was provided by the Indian Space Research Organization (ISRO). *Chandrayaan-I*'s mission is to orbit the Moon and collect information so scientists can redraw maps of the lunar surface.

Earth's atmosphere causes objects like meteors to burn up before they hit the planet's surface.

The huge planets farther away from the Sun's heat have gathered so many gases that their atmospheres are poisonous.

Earth's position in the Solar System makes it special in another way. The endless reaches of space may seem empty, but space is actually a crowded and dangerous place. Billions of objects, like the one that is believed to have collided with Earth to create the Moon, are constantly racing through space. Many of them have struck our planet over millions of years but other planets are struck more often. One reason is that Earth has developed an atmosphere that causes approaching bodies to "burn up."

The presence of other nearby bodies is another reason that Earth has been less affected by collisions with other celestial objects. The enormous gravitational force of the planet Jupiter—even though it is about 365 million miles (587 million km) away from Earth—seems to deflect asteroids and other bodies away from our planet. For example, in the early 1990s, a huge **comet** struck Jupiter. It left an impact site approximately the size of Earth. The comet was not on course to strike Earth, but if a body that size did hit Earth, it would probably destroy the entire planet.

Despite the gravitational influence of other heavenly bodies and the protective effects of the atmosphere, objects from space do strike the Earth regularly. Most are quite small, but some are huge and have an enormous impact on the planet. Many scientists believe that a huge asteroid that struck Earth about 65 million years ago—leaving a crater 125 miles (201 km) wide—may have been responsible for the extinction of the dinosaurs and as much as 70 percent of all life on Earth.

Deep craters of many different sizes can be found on all parts of the Moon. Many of the craters are named after different scientists.

THE MOON'S INFLUENCE

The Moon's gravity also seems to lead other bodies away from Earth and toward its own scarred surface. The Moon has an influence on Earth in other, subtler ways. One of these influences is on the ocean tides. Scientists believe that life on Earth first emerged in the oceans, and the tides are probably one of the most important reasons. As the Moon moves closer to Earth in its orbit, the Moon's gravity pulls the ocean toward it, raising the water level. Biologists believe that this regular, predictable rising and falling of the oceans every few hours created an environment where life-forms could evolve. This early life probably experimented with life on land for a few hours at a time before returning to the safety of the ocean.

The Moon's gravity helps to keep Earth stable, in terms of both the planet's axial tilt relative to the Sun and its overall orbit. The Moon is probably also responsible for another key factor in the emergence and survival of life on Earth—the planet's stable 23.5-degree axial tilt relative to the Sun. This stable tilt, which is probably the result of the collision with Theia that likely created the Moon, allows our planet to have a broad range of stable, relatively unchanging climate zones, from the frozen areas of the North and South Poles to the hot tropical zones. This diversity of climate zones has probably helped the broad range of complex life-forms, including mammals such as humans, to emerge and evolve over billions of years. Without the stable tilt, the planet would be too hot and too cold for too long, making life difficult or even impossible.

Another surprising effect that the Moon has on Earth is the presence of metals. Earth has a lot of metallic rock close to the surface, where it can be mined and used in almost everything human beings make, from cars to computers. Physicists and geologists theorize that much of this metallic content used to be deep in the mantle, but was dragged to the surface by the Theia impact. Studies of rocks from the Moon have shown that the Moon's mineral content is very similar to Earth's in many important ways. Scientists are beginning to believe that the Moon contains valuable resources—resources that could someday be used here on Earth. This belief is causing increased interest in returning to the Moon—something that was not being considered just a few years ago.

Without the Moon's gravitational pull, the oceans' waters would not move.

RETURNING TO THE MOON

After the last three *Apollo* missions were canceled, NASA focused its attention on other space missions. But in 2004, the United States government announced a new plan to return to the Moon by 2020. NASA plans to launch an unmanned exploration mission in 2009 to explore places where humans could land and possibly even live for extended periods of time. One place of special interest is the Shackleton crater, near the Moon's south pole. Scientists suspect that there could be traces of water there. In 2008, researchers from Brown University in Rhode Island found the first evidence of water deep inside the Moon, and scientists are very anxious to find out whether significant amounts exist.

However, the United States is not the only country interested in renewed exploration of Earth's satellite. Russia plans to launch an unmanned mission that will both orbit and land on the Moon in 2012. Other countries that did not take part in the original space race are planning their own lunar projects. On October 22, 2008, India launched *Chandrayaan-1,* an unmanned spacecraft that will orbit the Moon for two years, taking clearer images and preparing for *Chandrayaan-2*, which is a mission designed to land a rover on the lunar surface in 2011. China also plans to place a rover on the Moon, probably around 2012, and Germany has plans for lunar exploration, as well.

An illustration shows a manned Moon spacecraft that will be built by the Japanese Aerospace Exploration Agency (JAXA). They hope to launch the spacecraft in 2020.

Most exciting of all, other countries are planning to send human beings to the Moon. The Japanese Aerospace Exploration Agency (JAXA) has announced that it intends to send a manned mission to the Moon by 2020 and establish a base there by 2030. The European Space Agency's *Aurora* program also plans to send human beings back to the Moon.

Exploring the Moon is no longer something that is being left to countries and their governments. Even businesses and nonprofit organizations are becoming involved. Google, the Internet search provider, announced the Google Lunar X Prize, a twenty-million-dollar award for the first successful private mission to the Moon. Other companies are considering the possibility of using some of the Moon's resources to solve problems here on Earth—and to make money at the same time. The object of their most intense interest is a gas called helium-3.

Alternative Energy from the Moon?

The Sun produces helium-3 in huge amounts and sends it far into space on the solar wind. Our planet's atmosphere and magnetosphere prevent it from reaching Earth. Scientists have found large amounts of it concentrated in the Moon's rocks, probably because the Moon's limited atmosphere cannot stop it. (It is probably found on other planets, as well.) Helium-3 can be used to create energy, but it is so rare on Earth that it has not been a practical power source.

Some scientists believe that 1 pound (0.45 kilograms) of helium-3 could replace almost 5,000 tons of fossil fuels, such as oil and coal. If they are right, 1 ton (0.9 tonnes) of helium-3 could produce enough electricity to power a city of 5 million people for an entire year. Some estimates suggest that there may be as much as 1 million tons (0.9 million tonnes) of helium-3 on the Moon. If scientists could figure out a way to bring that back to Earth, it could be enough to power the entire world for a thousand years.

The promise of a new power source, one that could reduce the world's dependence on oil and other fossil fuels, is behind a new kind of space race. Companies in both the United States and Russia are investing billions of dollars in ambitious plans to mine helium-3 on the Moon and transport it back to Earth for use as a fuel. It would not be easy, and it would not be cheap.

Perhaps someday this lunar view of the rising Earth will be a normal sight for people living and working on the Moon.

©JAXA/NHK

NASA estimates that the cost of keeping one person on the Moon would be one million dollars per minute!

Many people believe that the Moon should not be used in this way. They think this precious satellite should be preserved and used only for exploration and scientific discovery. However, the pressure to use the Moon to help solve some of Earth's problems may be too strong for humankind to resist.

The idea of human beings living on the Moon, and perhaps using the Moon's resources to help solve Earth's energy problems, may seem far-fetched. But not so long ago, space exploration also seemed like a fantasy, something for science fiction writers and other dreamers. We do not know exactly what the future of human beings on the Moon will be, but it seems clear that we are going back to the Moon at last, to learn more about this, our most important neighbor.

QUICK FACTS ABOUT EARTH AND THE MOON

Earth

DIAMETER: 7,926 miles (12,756 km)

AVERAGE DISTANCE FROM SUN: 93 million miles (149.6 million km)

LENGTH OF DAY: 23.93 hours

LENGTH OF YEAR: 365.25 days

ATMOSPHERE: Mostly oxygen and nitrogen, but other elements are also present

COMPOSITION: Mostly metallic rock, with large areas covered with water

NUMBER OF MOONS: 1

Moon

DIAMETER: 2,160 miles (3,476 km)

AVERAGE DISTANCE FROM EARTH: 238,900 miles (384,400 km)

AVERAGE DISTANCE FROM THE SUN: 93 million miles (149.6 million km)

LENGTH OF DAY: 27.3 Earth days

LENGTH OF YEAR: 27.3 Earth days

ATMOSPHERE: Very thin, with water and tiny amounts of gas including neon, helium, and hydrogen

COMPOSITION: Mostly metallic rock, with extremely limited water

GLOSSARY

astronomer—A scientist who studies space and the objects in it.

asteroid—A small celestial body, made mostly of rock, which travels around the Sun in a highly elliptical orbit.

atmosphere—A layer of gases that surrounds a planet or other celestial body.

axis—An invisible line running down the center of a celestial object. Planets and other celestial objects often rotate, or spin, on an axis.

axial tilt—The angle of one object (such as a planet or moon) in relation to something else.

celestial object—A body in space.

comet—A small body, made of rock, dust, and ice, that orbits around the Sun in a highly elliptical orbit.

dwarf planet—A celestial body orbiting the Sun that is massive enough to be rounded by its own gravity but has not cleared its neighboring region of planetesimals and is not a satellite.

eclipse—A period when either the Sun or the Moon is temporarily blocked from view.

elliptical—Following a regular, rounded path that is not a perfect circle.

equinoxes—The two times a year when the periods of light and darkness on Earth are equal.

galaxy—A huge revolving cluster of stars and other bodies and matter.

gravity—An invisible force that attracts one body to another.

impact crater—A mark left on a celestial object by the impact of another celestial object.

light-year—The distance that light travels in one year.

lunar—Having to do with the Moon.

lunar cycle—The changing appearance of the Moon over the course of a month.

lunar eclipse—A brief period when Earth comes between the Sun and the Moon, causing the planet to throw a shadow on the Moon.

magnetosphere—An area of magnetic force around a celestial object.

maria—Flat, dark areas on the Moon's surface.

mass—The amount of matter an object contains.

matter—The substance of which something is made.

meteoroid—A small body that moves through space. It is called a meteor if it enters Earth's atmosphere, and a meteorite if it reaches Earth's surface.

moon—A natural satellite that orbits a planet.

National Areonautics and Space Administration (NASA)—The space exploration agency of the United States government.

observatory—A place or structure used to observe celestial objects.

physicist—A scientist who studies matter and energy.

planetesimal—A small body of matter formed by the creation of the Sun or other star.

radiation—Energy that is transmitted in waves or particles.

regolith—Loose, dusty rock found on the Moon's surface.

rover—A motorized vehicle, manned or unmanned, that is used to travel on the surface of a body in space.

satellite—An object, natural or manmade, that orbits an object in space, such as a planet.

silicate—One of a group of substances containing silicon, oxygen, and metals.

Solar System—The Sun and the billions of objects that orbit around it.

solar eclipse—A brief period when the Moon comes between Earth and the Sun, blocking the Sun's light.

solar wind—A stream of radiation constantly sent into space by the Sun.

solstices—The two times of the year when the most direct sunlight reaches Earth.

star—A huge ball of burning gas revolving in space. The Sun is a star.

terrestrial—Having to do with land. The terrestrial planets in our Solar System are Mercury, Venus, Mars, and Earth.

universe—All the matter and energy in existence.

FIND OUT MORE

BOOKS

Bell, Trudy E. *Earth's Journey through Space.* New York: Chelsea House, 2007.

Carson, Mary Kay. *Exploring the Solar System: A History with 22 Activities.* Chicago: Chicago Review Press, 2008.

Elkins-Tanton, Linda. *The Earth and the Moon.* New York: Chelsea House Publications, 2006.

Jefferis, David and Mat Irvine. *Return to the Moon.* New York: Crabtree Publishing, 2007.

Simon, Seymour. *Our Solar System.* New York: Scholastic, 2005.

Thimmesh, Catherine. *Team Moon: How 400,000 People Landed Apollo 11 on the Moon.* New York: Houghton Mifflin, 2006.

Vogt, Gregory L. *Earth's Core and Mantle: Heavy Metal, Moving Rock.* Brookfield, CT: Twenty-First Century Books, 2007.

WEBSITES

CoolCosmos: Earth
http://coolcosmos.ipac.caltech.edu/cosmic_kids/AskKids/earth.shtml

Earth and Moon Viewer
http://www.fourmilab.ch/earthview/vplanet.html

NASA Solar System Exploration for Kids
http://solarsystem.nasa.gov/kids/index.cfm

NASA Space Place
http://spaceplace.nasa.gov/en/kids

The Nine 8 Planets—Just for Kids
http://kids.nineplanets.org/earth.htm

Welcome to the Planets—Earth
http://pds.jpl.nasa.gov/planets/choices/earth1.htm

World Book at NASA for Students—Earth
http://www.nasa.gov/worldbook/wbkids/k_earth.html

World Book at NASA for Students—Moon
http://www.nasa.gov/worldbook/wbkids/k_Moon.html

BIBLIOGRAPHY

The author found these sources especially helpful while researching this book.

Fothergill, Alastair. *Planet Earth: As You've Never Seen It Before.* London: BBC Books, 2006.

Frances, Peter. *Universe: The Definitive Visual Guide.* London: Dorling Kindersley, 2006.

Harland, David M. *Exploring the Moon: The Apollo Expeditions.* New York: Springer-Praxis, 2006.

Illustrated Encyclopedia of the Earth. London: Dorling Kindersley, 2009.

Kerrod, Robin. *The Star Guide.* London: Quarto, 2005.

Schyffert, Bea Usma. *The Man Who Went to the Far Side of the Moon: The Story of Apollo 11 Astronaut Michael Collins.* San Francisco: Chronicle Books, 2003.

Time Magazine (Editors). *Time Planet Earth: An Illustrated History.* New York: Time Inc. Home Entertainment, 2008.

INDEX

ABOUT THE AUTHOR

Terry Allan Hicks has written more than twenty children's books, about everything from why people catch colds to how mountains form. He lives in Connecticut with his wife, Nancy, and their three sons, James, Jack, and Andrew.